Our Mind and Spirit

(2005)

*

essay

*

Traumear

Paperback ISBN 978-0-244-48576-4

*

www.traumear.com

*

**Some of the themes
followed up in this discursive essay:**

Our mind, visible or invisible – thought as responsible
activity both human-natural and spiritual – true thought –
knowing the truth as useful – awareness vs. consciousness –
escape from the trap of things – thought as good spirit –
the human need to learn – wisdom as fulfilment – thought and
cerebration – inspiration – reason and faith – link of mind
with flesh, brain with body – thinking as aid out of immaturity
– art as spiritual – the spirit of humility, of greed etc. –
abiding in the spirit of truth –
the messianic spirit.

*

Our Mind and Spirit

It would take some time to chart the development of the human mind – especially if one knew what was meant by that. Allegedly our mind is located somewhere in our head. It is a head function. Is it a function? Of what? Is my mind a function of my will to think, or is my thinking a function of my mind?

It's all speculation, really; an attempt to come to terms with what we use our heads for, allegedly so that we can do it better. The trouble starts when we try to think about thinking. Best to avoid that trouble from the start. Next we would be feeling our feeling. Dreadful! Nonetheless it goes on all around us. I do it myself sometimes, inadvertently. I apologize.

To make it less likely that I will ever think about thinking again, anywhere, on the street, at my work, in my sleep – I propose to 'show thought' and to show what it means to think. Spirit, by comparison, is not so readily shown. Nonetheless, a soon as spirit comes into it, my mental faculties – how shall I put it – are no longer what they were.

Spirit has a way of making me dance, of making me leap, whirl, stand stock still with a vengeance, that sort of thing. Right at this moment I depend on spirit to move me and to sort me out. I am not master of this spirit. It seems to be more or less the other way around. So this too has to be carefully considered.

Many questions suggest themselves. I take nothing for granted now but look at everything to do with mind and spirit anew. The human mind; my mind; 'the' mind; spirit, the human spirit, divine spirit; the spirit of the times, of the world; good spirit, evil spirit. Spirits! The spirit of Jesus.

What is a spiritual man? What does it mean to be inspired? Can we be inspired by a variety of spirits? 'Inspiration', we say, and seem to mean something. God is spirit, but not 'the' spirit. Where does one start? So many questions, so little clarity! The twenty-first century – bag-loads of mail arrive on the doorstep,

1

innumerable questions, requests for questions or just plain requests for quests. Show me somewhere to go, anywhere. I can see no reason for moving from A to somewhere else; certainly I have no notion of B or even C.

*

I watch a man. I observe how he walks; he shuffles along, head forward, the arms loose in the joints. He walks on the balls of his feet. When he comes to a halt, he does so as if he had to steady himself with his hands. He speaks to a woman, as if he were accusing her. Look how he laughs now. Look how he takes her by the elbow and steers her across the street. I mean this precisely: Look how he does that. He does not offer her his arm and guide her across. He doesn't drag her across by the hair. He is neither forceful nor gentlemanly. He does it awkwardly and surely she could get away from him if she chose. Ah, there, she frees herself now, swaggers away from him. He is left standing. For a few seconds he looks after her, shouts something, then heads off in the opposite direction. I believe I saw him shake his head.

To some extent we are able to separate what he did from how he did it. We can describe how he behaved without speculating why he behaved like that. He moved in a way that revealed how he was at that time. He was not particularly intent on disguising how he was; he was only minimally posing.

The 'how' of his being, behaving and doing, that is his mind, his mentality. The visibility of it is all there is to it. Mind you, that is quite a lot. If we want to become better acquainted with his mind, with what his mind is, we have to pay closer attention. We see, hear, taste, smell and touch someone's mental being and doing. We envision it. It is visible.

Let's be clear about he following: A visible mind is owned. The one who has this mind is responsible for it and willingly so, even gladly so. A mind worth referring to and talking about is in someone's care. Otherwise there is no mind. A visible mind is a human-natural possession. Even as we give ourselves over

2

to thought, we must be aware we are doing this, otherwise we are merely at the mercy of the elements. However the elements are merciless. Is this a roundabout way of saying what is obvious?

A masterful person's mind is most obvious for anyone who has eyes to see. As we become more masterful our mind becomes more distinct, more incapable of malfunction.

The first stirrings of mental activity can be observed in some-one, in a child for example, during those moments of stillness when it appears as if that someone is being guided. An absence of mind, by comparison, is signalled at a time of self-expression and self-assertion, when an individual is mechanically driven while insisting most adamantly, in his manner if not his word, on independent authority. In the former case good spirit is en-tertained by a person, while in the latter case an individual is being elementally motivated, or driven.

What is being revealed to us here is that a mind sound and proper involves good spirit. The elements, or elemental being, is absorbed by a mind. The urges and drives, of which we can be aware, are not resisted mentally by us during the growth and activity of our mind. They are its raw materials.

This highlights the fact that our mind is not a description of a state but it is a fruitful process. Whether we view it from within or from without, that is to say: whether we view real mentality from within, as within ourselves, or from without, as without our-selves and within someone else, it is nothing in itself but rather a contributory factor to something beyond itself, even as action contributes to a final achievement or work. This is where the ex-pression 'a rational mind' and 'a logical mind' begins to make sense.

*

The human mind could be described, then, as a creative trans-formation of elemental reality under the guidance of good spirit. Elemental reality is required as raw material and good spirit must be involved so that true thought may take shape. If we

3

can think of our mind as something going on and as something being done, we will get away from that false notion of it as an instrument or a tool. 'Use your mind' must mean something like: 'Institute a process, participate in an event'. The spiritual eventuality of our mind must be known about by us or we will continue to fall back on wilful thinking and on thinking separate from reality, which should be called something else but that is quite often what is meant by thinking, namely this harnessing of the brain for the purpose of filling in the gaps between fearfully disparate elements and calling them connections or relations. Also, that thinking must proceed, or rather quite simply that it does proceed, should not surprise us. Elemental reality after all is a flux. We are naturally embedded in elemental reality, like the foetus floating in amniotic fluid, so we must expect impulses and stimuli from there. They may be motivational or arresting. In other words, due to our elemental make-up we may be urged to proceed but we may also be persuaded just plain to cede, in the sense of letting something or someone else proceed.

*

Mind originates within us, spirit without. We can have mind without spirit but not spirit without mind. That is just about all we can say about mind and spirit before we have to ask: What mind? Whose mind? What kind of spirit? Since mentality goes on in the head it cannot be an isolated activity. Head and heart crave mutual connection. With that in mind, we should be able to discover how actual thinking begins. Anytime I wish I can take responsibility for this head activity, whereupon quite a lot changes. Mental pictures no longer figure. Also I am no longer convinced for a time that I am doing anything because nothing any longer goes on. A crowded or a troubled mind for which I take the responsibility is no longer crowded or troubled. That something creative does go on meanwhile has to be learned and known by me or simply accepted as a fact. There is no proof of this. What may seem like empty-headedness to me does so only in comparison to a previous head full of nonsense. Now that the nonsense is gone, what must I do to instigate thought? Nothing. I am thinking already.

What about thought as a problem-solving activity? The modern mind is rigged out with problems and proud of it. As soon as I accept the responsibility for the activities in my head, my problems are solved and I am thinking. I may continue to think as long as I like, which means as long as I keep my head responsibly clear, which means clear of nonsense.

Of course it doesn't appear to me as nonsense while I'm involved with it, attached to it, in charge of it; beset by it and so on. I would resent, at such times, having it described to me as nonsense. So much of my identity depends on irresponsible head content that any disparagement of it threatens my identity and that is terrible. My identity, after all, is what saves me from having to look too closely at what goes on in my head. Take my identity away, so it must seem to me, and what goes on in my head will be revealed to me as nonsense. Or – challenge the fundamental meaning of it, of this irresponsible activity, this business, and you threaten my identity. Due to my identity I am identical with others and do not, for the time being at least, have to break my head over what in reality I amount to.

Identity aside, what is being revealed to us here is that thinking goes on human naturally while we do not interfere with it and then, in addition to this we can give it our assent. We can say: Yes, I am in favour of this, I am grateful for it, I cooperate with it.

In other words we should refer to thought and to thinking in the following way: Thought is what goes on human-naturally until we interfere with it and thinking is what we do when we assent to thought and cooperate with it.

When we have cleared our head of all nonsense, we are in thought. This is sustainable for a while but then we either show we are in favour of this and make some kind of a thoughtful move or else nonsense reasserts itself and before we know it we even mistake it for meaningful sense.

We have a mind and we are in our right mind as soon as we cooperate with thought. We lose our mind as soon as we get involved with the nonsense that clutters the head and seems to amount to anything worth thinking about.

To be in thought and to be thoughtful, this is of the first order. We achieve this by clearing our head, by ridding ourselves of mental business when elemental raw materials are pressing and piling in on us. Now what is it like to assume or accept responsibility for this? It does require a degree of knowledge, I suppose. Young children are often quite good at it but we adults usually have to reclaim territory. We have to say: This is my fault that I am mixed up and in turmoil. This is not how it should be and not how it was in the beginning. It's entirely up to me whether I continue in this welter of prejudices, convictions and opinions all threaded together by uncertainty and self-esteem or else allow for human-natural thought, which is neither induced nor produced but it simply is. I humbly admit that I cannot even begin to think until I opt for the latter and so I have opted for the latter. There is no additional button to push.

*

Thought is at once human-natural and spiritual. No contradiction is involved here except insofar as we are possessed by prejudices which will not allow for spiritual human nature, or for human-natural spirit, which is the same.

Thought is spiritual inasmuch as it derives from merciful good spirit and it is human-natural in that we are born with it. Why should we not be born with that which is derived from merciful good spirit?

As soon as we begin to think now and to have a mind of our own, we could be described as immersing ourselves in that human-natural spirit, allowing it to affect us as it would and might.

6

*

Spirit is nothing we can lay our hands on but it does lay its hand on us. This can be quite a frightening experience, especially the first time. It stands to reason that prior to any experience of spirit we would get into the unfortunate habit of carnal being and of supposing ourselves to be carnal beings. It all depends on how we have been brought up, what we have been taught and what we have learned. Just as we can learn about Alaska without ever having been there, so that at least we believe that such a place exists, so we can also learn about spirit prior to any actual experience of it. Then, when we have experience of it, we recognize what we have learned previously. Just as we believe that Alaska exists, while we may not be so sure about places such as Narnia or 'the land of the free', so we may also believe that spirit exists, even though we have never been in personal contact with it. A great deal depends on those who inform us and introduce us to the thought of it. The thought of spirit is an important concept indeed. It is the way spirit informs and instructs us. It's up to us how we pick up on this information and whether or not we pay heed to the instruction and lend ourselves to it. A parental adult cannot do better than draw the attention of the young to the spiritual thought within them. What they learn from there, from within themselves, is by definition primarily effective. Training, by comparison, can be helpful.

The initial responsible activity, then, which allows us to refer to such an entity as 'our individuality' other than foolishly is a case of our paying heed to this spiritual thought. We can do that decisively. We can do it with a sense of purposeful application. The nonsense has been cleared from the head and we believe that spiritual thought exists and that it is available for us to address, within ourselves and in community with those at a similar or more advanced stage of development. Meanwhile of course we will not turn away those who are attracted by the possibility of thoughtful spirituality and would like help with having nonsense cleared from their heads so that thought will be revealed to them. Once we have made that crucial breakthrough ourselves, where thanks to a clear head we have actual experience of thoughtful spirit, we still have to maintain that state of clear-headedness, and the best way of doing it is by helping others to achieve it. Once we have an active mind, of course, we are much less likely to fall back into nonsensical head business. Nonetheless we can never afford to become arrogant.

There is the housecleaning and the homemaking. A good home maker does not have house cleaning as his priority but he will not neglect it, while he concentrates on home making. When a woman invites a guest into her house, her emphasis will be on courtesy, care and kindliness while not neglecting cleanliness and tidiness.

*

When I think, I participate in spiritual thought. Outward evidence of this is immediate. No one can think in a way that is not immediately perceivable from without.

Those who dispute this will no doubt come up with something like the hidden content of thought, but this has nothing to do with thought or with thinking. If I say to you think about a train and you agree to do so, you might picture a train in our head and you might recall a train or two you have seen and maybe piece together your own picture of a train. You can manipulate that picture as much as you like. A steam train is succeeded by an electric train, colour pink, quickly followed by one of those high-speed Japanese jobs that allegedly always arrive on time. Then you can stop picturing and recalling and manipulating pictures of trains as soon as you like, unless you are obsessive. All this, however, is something that happens to you and you either allow it to happen or you cannot help it. It would be wrong to call this something like passive thought, however. Thought, as we know it, is not involved. Nor can we call it 'thinking about' something, because all we are really doing is letting pictures enter our head and then we toy with them or we force them into some pattern. A kind of indistinct imagination plays a role, we might be able to say that much about it, but then we could say a whole lot about it if we had endless amounts of daytime and daylight. I am not being a spoilsport when I say: Turn away from it by choosing to think. I am merely suggesting we do something useful rather than waste our time and the time of those who are liable to be seduced by how cleverly and brilliantly we waste it.

What we are wise to get away from is any activity of 'mind on its own'. Only when we can call it truly our mind, I mine and you yours and we ours, is it really worth considering, but then it operates, in conjunction, at least, with our body. The more closely mind and body operate as one, the more truly are we entitled to speak of them as 'my' mind and 'my' body. certainly Heraclitus was moving in that direction when he employed the image of the drawn bow.

There is no middle way then. We either choose to think, to use our mind, which involves our body, or we allow ourselves to get caught up in what happens, instead. Our thinking can be improved, it can become powerful and above all loving, only to the extent that we leave behind and ignore all that accidental business which really requires carnal willing to manipulate and control it. The magician will show how perfectly he can control it and how masterfully he can manipulate it. Are we to admire him for wasting our time so expertly and for preventing us so successfully from developing and using our mind? If an entire culture or civilization were based on magic, well, so be it, does that mean we have to participate? Only those are not at liberty to think, who have given up their god-given right to do so.

They say they are free to think what they like but they do what they do in the dark and for that reason no one can stop them. He who truly thinks gives immediate evidence of it and those who prefer the darkness cannot see it. That makes good sense, doesn't it? Those who truly think do not hide what they think but those who prefer the darkness cannot see it. Thinking goes on in the light of day and those who think recognize one another. They are not recognized by those who prefer the darkness.

The fact that those who prefer the darkness cannot see that we think and what we think is no proof that mind and thought are invisible. Thought is visible inasmuch as we think and thinking is just plain visible. It is a loving activity and the more we love, the more are we able to think, and vice versa.

It is often hard to know what anyone means by 'pure thought'. Isolated head activity as a goal is a dangerous sport and one supposes it may be allowed to thrive for a time if only to demonstrate the pointlessness of it. Eventually the products of magical invention and those of magical destruction cancel each other out.

*

How do we 'show thought' then? By thinking. First we believe that thought exists and then, once we have experienced thinking, we know that thought exists and we can think as we wish.

Technically, no one can ever truly think what he likes. What he wishes, yes, but not what he likes. Unless, of course, he likes the truth. Is that possible? I might be worthwhile asking, is it possible to like the truth.

When you like something it is like you and you are like it. What is it you, and what or whom you like, have in common? It is an inclination, a tendency. You may not be consciously aware of that tendency. It happens that I like you but you dislike me. Nonetheless there must be a common inclination. I can also like apples but dislike pears. Can an apple like me, subconsciously even? It's a droll notion. (I hear people say the likes of: 'I like spinach but it doesn't like me.) If instead of inclination we say distribution, it begins to make more sense that I and the apple should have something in common which I and pears do not, at a given time. Liking, of course, happens. We happen to like some-one or something. When we like a lot we might call it love but incorrectly, unless in the meantime we have decided to ignore our inclination in favour of good will and beneficial intention.

Generally speaking, liking happens, loving is done.

What we have in common with what we like is a distribution of parts. We are partial to what we like. I as a whole person do not like but some part or parts of me incline or tend in a given direction in which there is a similar distribution of parts. I may like the look of a thing, maybe, but I cannot love the look of it. The look of it, the mere appearance of it, gives me only aspects of it; parts, in other words.

Really I shouldn't be ignoring the difference between things and beings. An apple is not just a thing but a being. I mean a tangible apple in reality now, not a figment of someone's imagination, someone who has never bitten into one. We cannot really appreciate beings as such unless we love them and love, remember, is more than intense liking. Not only more but something else.

This notion of a distribution of parts is worth entertaining for a spell. How many parts to a being? Innumerable parts. How many parts to a thing? Well, things don't really exist as such, as we know, because they are really beings we have so far rejected on account of our metaphysical ignorance in that department. Unless we make the special allowance of love, beings appear as things to us. I have worked that out in many ways elsewhere. So if I like a thing, must I not be a thing myself to some extent? At least to the extent of my liking? We can, as we know, become so attached to the world of things, to 'this world' as some call it, that personality and being don't get a look in.

We can see a bit better now how the distribution of the parts of a thing can coincide or not with the distribution of your or my parts. Which parts have come to the fore; which parts are prominent. It happens. There is no rhyme or reason to it except for the note we take of it and what we do with the information. There is only the one reason for taking note of what we happen to like or dislike, and that is so that we can love, and love intelligently, in an informed fashion. Both like and dislike let us know that love is now advisable. In both cases, of like and dislike, what has happened is an accidental contact of sorts and we do well not to ignore this. If we do, we become massive. Bigotry, class and race hatred, nationalism, egotism, fanaticism, all isms, really; in short all these combinations of like and dislike, are massive. An inarticulate partiality concurs with a self-expressed antipathy. I like my friends and hate my enemies. Well, of course! If my friends are those people I like, then I like my friends and if my enemies are those I dislike then I hate (dislike intensely) my enemies.

This lets me know that when I like I also automatically dislike, although not necessarily at the same precise moment. If I am black and like black people, I will to that extent dislike whites, or non-blacks. I am thinking this through carefully and not leaving it to conventional manners of talk and behaviour. That's what philosophy is about, after all. If someone likes manipulating concepts, that does not amount to philosophy. He has to love knowledge. – I only partly digress.

This teaching of the distribution of the parts of a being or thing is not so important. It only helps to affirm the difference between liking and loving and to confirm our knowledge of the accidental nature of liking and disliking.

Unlike the truth, like and dislike depend on accuracy and correctness. Something is *simply* true but *more or less* accurate and correct. The simple truth is not massive, it does not depend on how many people like it and how much they like it, but it is personal and communal; persons and communities depend on the truth. The masses depend on what they like and dislike.

Is that the truth? Have you ever noticed how we refer to 'the' truth? We don't refer to 'the' falsehood. Or to 'the' nature. The sun, yes, the earth, the moon, the stars. Not the star. The Rocky Mountains? The United States of America – no, those are qualified. Like the star of Bethlehem. Can it also work the other way around? The moons of Jupiter. The moon is a satellite. The earth's moon is a satellite. Jupiter has at least thirteen. While I think there is only one moon I call it 'the' moon. When another one turns up I have to specify, is that it? Is that all there is to it? God is God and I'm a fanatic? There are as many gods as you like, my friend, let's be reasonable. "I am God and thou shalt have none other before me." The truth is relative. There is the criminal's truth, the idiot's truth, the plumber's truth, the artist's truth. "I am the truth, the resurrection and the life." Catch yourself on, man. How can you be so sure of that? There might be many more than one human nature. Oh really? More than one reality? One world? There is the truth of the juggler of concepts. He entertains us. Let's not depend on him for our spiritual nourishment. For that we need absolutes. All is relative; yes, that is absolutely true.

To what shall we compare the truth? A man walked out one morning and came upon a pond where he gazed at his reflection in the water. Then he looked up at the sun and behold, it looked into him and awakened him to his nature. He was not the same man who walked home.

Or again, a woman took care of her house and turned it into a home so that all who lived therein might be comfortable. One day a great storm blew up and destroyed that house, so the woman was given a tent and she took care of it and turned it into a home, a comfort for all who lied in it and that home was the same as the one before.

*

When we know the truth we do something useful. It takes time. How do we know it's the truth we know? How do we know we are doing something in the first place rather than merely blotting up impressions indiscriminately until they overwhelm us in some way?

We might be able to walk into town absentmindedly, while thinking about something else or not thinking at all but we won't know the truth except in the fullest possible awareness of what we are doing. This 'fullest possible awareness' has to be practiced, of course. We have to train our mind, discipline it. Rubbish continually tends to intervene. We call it rubbish only because it gets in the way of disciplined mental awareness. We call shepherd's purse a weed, but only when it gets in among the lettuce too plentifully.

Awareness is prime mind time. Not only do you know what you're doing when you're aware but you are doing something useful. If you are doing something wasteful and you become aware of it you stop. Turn on awareness and you turn off abuse. Aim for that. Try to get your mind to that pitch where it becomes capable of this essential mental activity; this essentially mental activity. Don't confuse it with consciousness now, we will come around to that.

Something to keep in mind about awareness is that we do not arrive there in stages. What I mean is: We don't notice, then notice more carefully, then observe more accurately until we become conscious, then more and more conscious until awareness sets in. No. Awareness is the spark called true mind. The newborn babe is aware. We are born human-naturally into the light of day and are perfectly aware. There is no reason under the sun why we should not remain aware. Alas! We are brought up and educated in ways that lead away from the truth of this mental faculty rather than remaining in line with it.

Awareness is mind in its true form, not divorced from the body. Always keep in mind that I look at this from the point of view of mind and body as one. Not from an adolescent point of view but from a mature one do we learn and understand usefully. Technically both knowledge and understanding coincidentally testify to this marriage of body and mind, even though each

14

one may at any one time lean more to one side and then to the other. I suppose that goes without saying.

Having sung the praises of awareness sufficiently, we can now take the next step. As we train our mind-awareness it becomes more powerful in the sense that we are able to deal with greater interruptions and above all else in that we are able to create order where there is disorder. Whether our mind, or we, or our life becomes disorderly, awareness powerfully creates order. We create order by being more powerfully aware.

This lets us know that being aware involves thought. Remember that we participate in thought when we think and that thought is spiritual. By being aware we make it possible for truthful spirit or thought to come into the world and in that way we make it available for others in one way or another and in one fashion or another.

This creation of order is therefore a fundamental human-natural activity. The fact that this creation of order depends on awareness, on being aware and not on something called reason might be worth keeping in mind, because the fundamental order is not something we arrange in compliance with a plan or recipe we have previously worked out but it is always re-established, recreated; in other words that which causes, or has caused, disorder is removed. The terms 'old order' and 'new order' do not really apply because creation was initially, is now and always will be orderly, so all we can take credit for is management, in the widest sense of the word, of course. People will talk about the new and the old order, and about changing the world and one wonders is their own mind in order and do they possess a mind of their own. Can they guarantee a contribution of awareness or are they simply trying to manipulate circumstances and alter appearances because they have not yet seen to the possession of an orderly mind?

*

15

Mind is thought, is awareness, is orderliness. We take it for granted, when we use our mind, that the world will fall in with it. Our mental capacity and the world order stem from the same principle. It takes a little thinking to see the world in the round. Our mind and the world we live in stand in a peculiar relation to each other and we need to keep that in mind so that we will not lose courage when the world, so to speak, is against us.

Thought as we know it is world presence. When we come upon thought in ourselves the world changes completely. Where before it occurred to us, as masses of information shadowing forth a mysterious structure, now it is no longer merely 'there', but woven dramatically into our very knowledge and understanding.

This is why thought and thinking are so important, because of their relation to the world and the relation of the world to them. It is one principle that unites them. This principle is not available to us until and unless we think.

The world as masses of information, once again, is a thing and not a being. Saying it is a thing is like saying it is not, or not really. Our ambition therefore must be to ignore this thing long enough for us to learn how to think – or indeed we have lost the ability to think, which is quite likely if we have not been properly brought up and not rightly educated. As a child I was aware. There was a time when I had not lost contact with thought. As I grew up, what should have been done is that I should have been helped to become more consciously aware. As adults we are at liberty to think or not to think and for most this is a terrifying liberty. The choice to confront the world and one another, as persons, in other words, or else to become daily less aware and merely conscious, superficially conscious, instead, is placed in our hands during adolescence. We either become mature or immature.

This is not quite so simple as it sounds. There is the crucial fact to be considered that thought, this spiritual reality, asserts itself – draws painful attention to itself – insists on being taken into consideration, so that we might eventually after all mature and leave behind our immaturity. How readily we will make mature decisions during our adolescence depends on how well we were brought up and how thoroughly educated. With adulthood comes the opportunity then of adult education, when we ourselves have to take ourselves in hand and accept responsibility for any shortcomings in our personality and character – which is the same as to say: in our world view.

Always remember that education in truth is the correction of upbringing. When we look at it closely we come to realize that upbringing and education really run side by side as parental adults bring children to maturity. Upbringing is human-natural while education is art. Think of it like this: As we bring a child up we walk in front of that child in exemplary fashion, taking care that the child follows. The child must grow up at his own speed, so now and again is it not bound to happen that we move too rapidly or too tardily for that particular child? The child strays into the scrub by the side of the road or suddenly finds itself ahead of us. What counts therefore is the match between the parental adult's walk and the child's walk. The perfect upbringing, if we can imagine such a thing for the moment, obviates education. One can imagine children growing up normally because they are being brought up normally by mature adults, so that the art of education is never required. And it's quite true that imagination is important so that we know what to aim for in reality and so that our reality is not aimless. In reality then the art of education comes into its own.

It should also be mentioned here that upbringing and education are at home in our home. Where parental adults create a home for themselves and their children, state education is not necessary. This is also important to know, that the State is not crucial. What is crucial is home and community. The State comes into being and steps in where community fails and the home is neglected.

17

The true image of school, by comparison, is one of adults voluntarily getting together during their leisure hours for the purpose of adult education. They would confess an immaturity and seek to update their effectiveness as mature members of their community and therefore also as parental adults. School for children is something like an official correction centre and the upshot of it seems to be an unwillingness by adults to confess and deal with their immaturity and blaming children for it. One wonders that children have stood for it so long, but of course they can be coerced and bullied. Home life and community environment is what children need on their way to maturity. Until adults have seen to these they should not take it upon themselves to have children.

When we look at how adults generally spend their time and how they fill their leisure hours, is it any wonder that children find it hard to be human beings? They are born with the human natural predisposition for maturity and wherever they turn they are treated like mechanical monsters. No wonder, since we ourselves have become mechanical monsters, with our emphasis on mere survival and our ignorance of life!

A mature human being is at rest, with a surplus of leisure time. During that time he is at liberty to choose freedom. He chooses to think, to use his mind for the furtherance of humanity and in the interest of community. He lives where he does and that is the country he lives in and while he chooses freedom, statehood and nationality and political government are as irrelevant to him as a zoo or a circus to an animal in the so-called wild. While he uses his imagination he has no need for idealism. Ideals pertain to the realm of art in any case. Their relevance is to the construction of art works and not to the leading of life. Art cannot be effective for life unless a clear distinction is maintained between the two.

*

Thought, we have said, painfully asserts itself. This fact must be seen in conjunction with the one that both world and mind stem from the same principle. Thought is spirit and world is the creation of that spirit. The same spirit is active within and without us. We ourselves are at liberty to unite ourselves with that spirit and to the extent that we do we are free. Both outwardly and inwardly we may secure our being and confirm our doing.

Any comparison of mind and spirit, of thought and awareness, leads naturally to the supposition of consciousness, which affords us the ability to step back for a moment in impersonal fashion. Probably less is known about consciousness than about any other human faculty and considering the nature of the case, this is perfectly understandable. For one thing, consciousness cannot be 'known about', because it itself is what permits us to 'know about' this and that. For another, the great sense of liberty we experience during moments or periods of consciousness misleads and seduces us to try to take hold of consciousness itself, so that we might always be at liberty and forever be at greater and greater liberty. It is as if we fell in love with liberty and must therefore ascertain for ourselves a permanently effective consciousness, without which liberty is unthinkable.

The tragedy here is typically that the more we make of liberty, the less are we capable of freedom. The difference between liberty and freedom is never concealed to the awareness of a mature mind. When we think, we cannot help but know that while we think we are passing from liberty to freedom, from mere or seeming freedom to true and real freedom.

Knowledge of the limits of consciousness is crucial. Consciousness, not to be confused with awareness, has a limited application or use. Just as money cannot gain us blessedness, so can consciousness not gain us freedom. Money can, however, gain us happiness, but happiness lasts for a little while. In the same way can consciousness gain us liberty but liberty in itself is temporary. Just as we might say to one man: Look, you have bought for yourself much land, a large house and you have a beautiful wife but you are no longer happy – so we might say to another man: Look, you know about the perfectibility of man, the relativity of the law and the causality of the world but you are no longer at liberty! Why is that? The one man confuses happiness with blessedness, the other liberty with freedom.

Neither, or course, do we have to be happy and at liberty before we can have blessedness and freedom. This is a serious and sad mistake made by those who do have an inkling of blessedness and a glimpse of freedom. However the foretaste of the reality is not the reality and an insistence on more and more foretaste does not gain us reality.

Consciousness is like a light that temporarily shines on us so that we might become aware of our abilities and use them. In the light of consciousness we may prepare ourselves for freedom. Consciousness is like a spotlight that indicates for us new areas of application, other opportunities for increase. We cannot apply consciousness or cause it to increase.

For our study of our mind and spirit specifically it matters that we do not mistake consciousness and liberty for ends in themselves.

*

It is our own mind with which we think and then we are free. Freedom implies thought coming into the world. Human beings cannot help but struggle until they are free. Consciousness, liberty, happiness are not necessary for human being. To be human implies a need for thought.

We do well to take care how we use such words as mind and mental, especially at a time when the modern constellation of mind, body and soul is no longer applicable to life in the light of day – if indeed it ever was! We speak of mental illness all too often as if we knew what we meant when in fact all we mean is a disturbed or inappropriate consciousness. If a clinging to consciousness in the light of awareness is the problem, should that rate as mental illness? Is it not what we would expect if we were the least bit less mercenary and more merciful?

The attempt to take hold of consciousness and to wield it, as a tool or instrument, even as a weapon, and the desire to become conscious of everything and then rest on the Sabbath to beat all Sabbaths, this is perfectly understandable too, precisely because consciousness liberates us from the contradictions of our mortal existence.

In truth what happens is that our two-dimensional existence is challenged so that the contradictions of it are revealed to us in the light of consciousness and at the same time we are given a glimpse of real, three-dimensional existence, in which those contradictions no longer occur. That we have to come up with awareness now, in order to realize this three-dimensionality, this cannot be naturally obvious to us. It has to be learned. The need for awareness has to be learned. Who will teach us: well, I, for example am telling you right now. Does that mean you are bound to accept what I say?

Not at all. You are at liberty to reject this teaching, along with any others, and to insist on consciousness, as a faculty, by means of which you will time and again seek to cause and manage your liberty in such a way that the obvious (due to that consciousness!) contradictions will be smoothed out. The fact that your effort is in itself contradictory would have to be taught to you but you reject this teaching and instead produce wonders of 'scientific progress' until you have tired yourself out.

The very notion that the light of consciousness, this forerunner of awareness, can be acquired and managed is, of course, faulty. No matter how exuberantly and superabundantly conscious we are, this is still, and always will be, a transient energy with which we are blessed for the purpose not of discovering the otherwise concealed laws, forces and mechanisms of 'nature' but rather to highlight our need of awareness.

Then why is it so difficult to take this step from consciousness to awareness and why do so few take it? It may be due to our preference for pleasant, self-generated solutions and our reluctance to learn from one another. Indeed our education system, although there is much talk of teaching and learning, mostly passes on endless repeats of pleasant, self-generated solutions to problems that could actually be called problems of awareness. Time and again our shortfall in terms of community is highlighted for us and the satisfaction we gain from self-aggrandizement allows us to suppose we have made headway when in fact we have only altered a few world appearances and produced a few more 'things'.

It takes great humility to escape from this trap. But humility is not and never will be popular. What is popular is the promise and the attempt to possess the world. It's all the same whether we try to corner the market in tinned baked beans or knock ourselves out to set up and uphold a 'Universal Church'. Imperialism imperils no one so much as the imperialist. What is popular is a massive work force to achieve massive goals – all in the name of a final, eternal liberty; which is like a great shop full of goodies which no one is allowed to purchase.

The unwillingness, or at least the unreadiness, to make room for that essentially human trait called humility, is what misleads into popularity, into the exaggeration of consciousness at the expense of awareness. When we get together with others in the interest of prolonged consciousness, we put our very humanity at risk. What in the case of awareness simply works out as a case of picking up our cross, our happiness and unhappiness, and carrying it, so that it becomes a burden easily borne, turns out, in terms of consciousness, as a corporate attempt to avoid burdens by making others, who are les conscious, carry them. It's all the same, again, whether it amounts to a tax burden or to a burden of guilt. In that case the conglomerates know how to make 'the little guy' pay the taxes and in this case the upper echelon of self-consciously 'good men' know how to pass the guilt on to 'the man on the street'.

But let's not confuse the light of consciousness with man's misguided attempts to lay hold of it and to operate with it. For the ego all it takes is a little happiness and it sees itself as master of the world. As we become conscious, which is like saying: conscious of our liberty or of ourselves as at liberty, we can do as we please. This is the defining characteristic of the political goal: to be at liberty to do as one pleases. If it should please us to tread on the person next to us as we revel in our liberty, we opt for a temporary state of being, since before long we ourselves will be trodden on, though very likely in some unforeseeable fashion. If instead it should please us to help the one next to us to his feet or at least to realize that the light of consciousness and its resultant liberty and happiness are something for which it suits us to be grateful, then the secret of awareness is in our grasp and we stand not far from freedom.

Human beings are forever learning. They are never of the opinion that all may be known. They know that knowledge is not like that. In truth consciousness is given us so that we might come to terms with knowledge as finite bites out of an infinite whole, not so that we will let it go to our heads.

Some are blessed in the sense that they could not abuse consciousness if they tried and their only option is awareness or unawareness. Those who abuse consciousness describe these blessed ones as mentally ill. Is mental illness not rather brought on by this abuse of consciousness? If those who only have the choice of awareness are made miserable by those who abuse consciousness, let them look to their misery for the key into awareness. They will learn how to become clever as snakes and guileless as doves. Divine humanity stands ready for such as these.

*

It's easy enough to imagine that our mind is what we have when we unite ourselves with thought and think. The fact that

23

this can be imagined, of course, tells its own story. We have also indicated that thought is spiritual. However, in what way is it spiritual? We have long ago learned that being spiritual is not necessarily a recommendation. Only observe how much spirituality nowadays races down the hill to throw itself into the lake and that is at least the end of it. So once again discernment is essential.

Now thought is good spirit alright and not just any spirit that is liable to enter our consciousness and take us over. In addition to that it is good spirit that has been learned and acquired. What we need to look at closely therefore is this business of learning. Perhaps we have gone to school and 'learned' that three fours make twelve and that the capital of Italy is presently Rome. That is of course useful and the more familiar we become with our environment the better. As long as the emphasis is on increased intimacy and familiarity, we do well to find out as much as we can and to share what we have found out. Look, it appears that this particular kind of snail prefers to eat that particular kind of mushroom. How interesting! We know that now and file it away. This is knowledge 'about'. It is familiarity with appearances. Appearances change. If that snail runs short of that particular kind of mushroom it will perhaps develop a taste for lichen and then its appearance will change, to blend in with the reindeer. Who can say? It's all very interesting. Like watching a movie. My goodness, look what this chap has come up with now! Wonderful! Greater familiarity does not breed contempt but it increases our sense of wonder. What *does* breed contempt is stupidity, which is due to a lack of openness to the world; or it is an openness only to the so-called magic of the world?

So we 'learn about' the contemporary appearances of the world and this helps us cope, so that we survive and then, when the bear and the tiger have been scared off and our patch of sweet potatoes is thriving we might take a moment or two to marvel at the way the sunlight reflects off the surface of the water and how our stick seems to bend under the water.

Survival tactics. Moments of leisure. None of this would work, would even be possible, if life did not creatively underpin it all; if life were not the essential common denominator; if life did not flow through it all and keep it up to the mark. Who says? Well, at the moment, I say. How do I know that this is so? I learned it. Why did I bother to learn it? Because it pressed itself upon me as something I ought to learn. When did I begin to learn this? In my early twenties, I suppose. I was a slow developer. Why do I tell you about it? Because that way I make room in myself so that I can learn a bit more. Also, communication is a real pleasure. The spirit we call life is essentially creative and existentially communicational.

It's certainly possible to imagine survival in the absence of any knowledge of life. It's the 'once upon a time' dream, the romantic utopia, the bucolic ideal. The fact that in down-to-earth reality the spirit that is life presses for recognition always and again, can successfully be imagined away, for a time. This is like a game in which we indulge our fancies. What a pity that in order to win this game – not that games necessarily need to be won – we are willing to make life miserable for the multitudes and to destroy half the earth while we're at it!

There you have it. The spirit that is life keeps pressing, keeps insisting on itself and we struggle against it because we have this notion that we might safely graze among our sheep and never a wolf in sight. Except that in the present case the wolf is life itself and how beneficial if we knew that!

We may know it. We can learn it. Then the pressure begins to make sense to us. The anxiety and the stress become reasonable. The panic, the rage, the guilt and shame all reveal themselves as the survival tactics of the spirit that is life, so that the only thoroughly intelligent behaviour is cooperative, not being aggressive, hostile and combative.

*

It's an musing suggestion that not I but life survives. When I concentrate solely on my own survival, at the expense of all sorts of other forms of life, life itself eventually presses in on me rather painfully, as if to say: Excuse me, haven't you forgotten something?

This expression: 'presses in on me', is evocative enough. 'I am heavily laden'. Do you like that better? "Come to me, you who are heavily laden," says life itself, "and I will make you whole".

Well, I believe we are into a learning situation there. I can imagine myself surviving but I cannot imagine life. To learn the ins and outs of life itself requires not imagination but fantasy. The realm of mystery opens up. The elders are seated on benches around a central altar. They are waiting for something to happen. Fire will descend from heaven and set the love-offering alight. They have to believe very strongly that this will happen or it won't. If it doesn't, they have only themselves to blame. They seek confirmation of the power of belief. Their faith is such that … ah, there! The flames! Gratitude wells up in their hearts. They suppress it. What would they be grateful for? That faith is what it is? That they have been able to come up with the goods? But are they not human beings, so what would you expect? Are they to be grateful for being endowed with opposable thumbs next? They had allowed the fire to go out. Oh how the community had suffered! It had been a cold, hungry winter. So they put their minds to it and spirit responded. Fair enough.

We learn first of all by believing that it's possible to learn. In our mind, by way of our thinking, we are able to make contact with good spirit, this we believe. Good spirit, or life, is open to suggestions. The correct approach is of the essence. What exactly are we after, we who are the children of the universe and whose god is current in our nerves and pulsates in our blood? Are we not after precisely this insight? Is that not what we want to learn?

We have some notion now of the learning process. I could not sit in a corner shut off from the world and come up with this. No, I must demonstrate an immediate readiness to impart to you and several others perhaps what I have learned before life-knowledge is vouchsafed me. It stands to reason, don't you think? I do not wish to become one of the learned, bloated with 'knowledge about' and empty of life. When we know life we certainly end up knowing nothing about it and that is how it should and must be. We can certainly fantasize about the 'nature' of life if we so wish and that can be like an entertaining game; on one side of the board the élan vital and on the other side a handful of clay, dry, lifeless. Your move. Glass pearls get shifted. Clay invents the abacus; a slowing-down tactic, no doubt. Élan vital condenses its breath over the drab surface of its 'opponent'. You see what happens as soon as we mention an opponent? Horns grow and hooves.

Well, this is the twenty-first century, after a manner of speaking, and we ought to try to learn what goes on here and now.

*

We can begin to learn whenever we wish. At first of course we will seem to ourselves singularly stupid. All of our faculties have been accustomed by us to the accumulation of survival tactics and now we are to make contact with life itself. We sit there defeated before we start, how can it be otherwise. It's as if our available organs had become hypnotized by cares about food and shelter, about the securities of the flesh. Probably we have been 'taught' that once our bellies are full, the rest will take care of itself. That there is a rest, and what this rest is, this has never been fully explained to us. The Lord of Money promises to deal with whatever should arise. We have come across examples in plenty of the foolishness that makes light of our 'need for essential necessities'; those who act as if the grapes and figs would drop into their mouths usually overlook that vineyards need to be tended and fig trees do not always bear fruit.

So we have to get away from the school of thought which separates spirit from nature. To learn life does not mean to ignore the belly, the roof and the climate. Neither does the tending of the vegetable patch imply neglect of the soul. As soon as we learn the least little bit of life we realize that this is so. What we call life and what deserves to be called life is all-inclusive on one hand and on the other it makes itself available to us both directly and indirectly, both inwardly and outwardly. Outwardly the world is replete and redolent with the spirit that is life. Inwardly our soul is alive and lively. Whether we turn inward or outward, life reveals itself. This is what it means to learn.

To turn inward or outward? Ah, so this means that ordinarily we do neither? Well, it's true, isn't it. Ordinarily we are both inwardly and outwardly intact. There's no question of turning one way or the other. I go for a walk through the wood on a summer's afternoon and take delight (inward) in observing the hush descending from the crowns of the trees (outward) while the twittering of the finches (outward) reminds me (inward) of a piece of music by Messiaen. I am at one with the world and at home in myself. I live. I have life. I have an abundance of it.

Now I want to learn. I have a choice. I choose to turn inward. In my patience I possess my soul. I ignore the world but only in the sense that all my faculties are for the time being taken up with my soul. A most unusual thing happens. I am abstracted and in my abstraction I am delivered of a series of insights. I record these. I do not ask what they mean but am assured of their meaningfulness.

As I turn towards my soul I am abstracted from the world for the time being and a series of meaningful insights is vouchsafed me. I am like one who speaks but does not yet know what he is saying. That is why I record what I come up with. More accurately, I come out with it, having first turned inward. I am learning. What I learn, because I record it, is right away available to others. If I were speaking, you might say I was 'speaking in tongues' and then an interpreter would be needed. However I am not speaking. No interpretation is required. It is simply that I am recording what I am inwardly learning and while I am recording it I am concerned with the truth and not the meaning of it. Afterwards, after a time, I may look at, or listen to, that record and then I will know what it means. Or let's instead say that some meaning will be possible and available for me, and for you too of course. A while later again there may be more of it.

You too, when you first look at my record, will wonder what it means. All true learning begins like that. First we are liable to wonder, does this have any meaning at all? We patiently expose ourselves to it and let it affect us. Because of the truth of it, the truth being one for all, we are able to trust it. We assume and believe that in the case of this particular record before us we may increase our knowledge of life and have more life in consequence. It may be hard for some, this particular record, and less hard, or downright easy, for others. It depends on who you are, on your predisposition, your inhibitions, etc. If you want to learn, you have something very specific in mind. Learning is not the same as entertainment, as playing, as celebrating and praising. It's work alright, but not all work is learning.

We can also learn by turning outward rather than inward.

*

By turning outward we learn in a different manner. Here we literally let ourselves be beguiled by the world, in the knowledge however that nothing can harm us from there. By this I mean that the world is entirely here for us, and not there. This naïve, simple, childlike approach to the world is productive of true wisdom.

Again, at first we may well have to overcome a degree of boredom. Leaning, outward as inward, is specific, is beyond the convention. We should expect that moment of boredom, when the world, or rather some aspect of it, occurs to us like a closed book, indeed precisely like something from which we cannot learn a thing.

This marks a decisive point. When we try to behold some aspect of the world and allow ourselves then to be put off by any kind of world-weariness we have simply not held out long enough. For how long and to what extent have we experienced the world as *there*, for example? To that degree our senses are prejudiced and our organs compromised. If we want to learn, all this has to be undone first. We will have to suffer the cleansing of our senses and the restitution of our organs, and that, like all suffering, takes time. So we do well to persevere to the point where the contemplation of world phenomena no longer tires us but leaves us with a sense of satisfaction and well-being. In many cases a rigorous discipline is required. It should be considered as the introductory part of the outward learning process.

The main part of the outward learning process is a period of contemplation, when we behold some aspect of the world in contentment and satisfaction. It is not insights we are vouchsafed now but examples. They are examples of reality. We set them down. We literally take them out of the mainstream of reality and set them down. This gives us great satisfaction and contentment and does the same for others who then contemplate what we have set down. Wisdom is above all else contentment and satisfaction. We experience fulfilment. We should not suppose that it can be gained with the aid of tools and instruments. What we must depend on are our own faculties and organs. What we perceive through spectacles, binoculars and telescopes is not outward reality. It is by way of our human-natural organs of perception that we learn outwardly.

It is among young children that we often come across the wisdom that is contentment and satisfaction and when this wisdom 'speaks' we have examples of reality. So what are we to think? Is learning the process by which we become like little children? Do we contemplate, specifically contemplate, aspects of the world so as to return to that same wisdom? If yes, we should perhaps ask how we have lost it since then? If reality is no longer mysterious for us as it was then, should we simply concentrate on re-conquering that sense of mystery which makes the world real or should we, as parental adults, also concern ourselves over how our children are most likely to lose that sense of mystery which is the essence of reality, so that with adulthood comes the nihilism which is the loss of soul and the inaccessibility to good spirit? Wisdom, as we know, is not first and foremost gained from books but it is sustained due to the process of resurrection which always and again empties us of an addiction to mortality and reconstitutes our immortality, so that we may be also, not essentially, mortal.

It is this addiction to mortality, where we like to interpret the world as a finite thing and as a collection of finite things, that depletes our child-wisdom. It gives us a little pleasure so we cling to this practice, as if it could compensate us for the loss of immortality. In that way the attempted remedy aids and abets the sickness.

*

The way out of the sickness of nihilism is by way of the annihilation of the self. It seems strange to talk about this as if one could set out to do it. Must we not wait for some shock from outside? And how can we possibly identify the self once we have so thoroughly become subject to it?

The human heart however is capable of its own restitution, so long as we do not interfere but assent to it. If thought is no longer accessible to us by an act of will, then we must rely on passion to see us through.

Are we able to identify the passionate impulse in ourselves? Can we say: Yes, here is the heart's defence against wilful abuse and therefore here also is the stronghold of the self, of the ever impertinent ego, which will not let us come to rest except that we first deal with it on its own terms and defeat it. The enemy in myself is the one who will give me no peace at the time when I most want it. He inhabits my mind and ostracizes it from the truth. He makes me fall asleep when I would wake and work and when I try to sleep he keeps me half awake with dreams. All the effort I have made so far to identify and overcome him have failed. I would be beguiled by reality but am betrayed by what poses as my mind. An incessant stream of pictures and noises draws attention to itself when I would prefer to attend to reality.

What is the main organ for perceiving reality? The human brain has evolved in such a way that many of its processes combine with mental processes so that we can think and cerebrate at one and the same time. Our passionate heart fuels these processes so that at times we do not know whether we think or are being thought. The whole procedure from beginning to end is called inspiration.

When we are inspired we cerebrate and think passionately. If we wrongly suppose our mind alone is involved we are liable to be influenced to our detriment, because brain impulses seem to take on an energetic identity of their own, so that we hear voices or see visions and run the risk of supposing them to be real. They are uninvested, or wild, brain impulses. Such impulses are initially inspirational and while we allow them to inform our thinking, so that we cerebrate and think at once, we create examples of reality.

Once again I would like to remind that our task is essentially cooperational. Organic activity always implies a voluntary dependence of the agent on influential spirit. Either the spirit invites and we accept the invitation or we register our desire and the spirit invariably responds.

Our ego cannot hold out in the face of organic inspiration. Where thoughtful and cerebral activity unite, the self is annihilated. The peace and rest we enjoy then is complete.

*

What do we mean, then, or at least what should we mean, when we say we are inspired? I have mentioned the three necessary elements, the thinking, the cerebration and the passion, and I have indicated that our attitude towards spirit, specifically good spirit, may be initiatory or receptive.

This attitude towards good spirit, or god, is perhaps least readily understood nowadays because of the apparent degree of expertise in our self-reliance. We have become capable of quite wonderful invention and discovery both inside and outside ourselves and to that extent, that we suppose we can nearly do anything and nearly know everything, good spirit cannot get through to us and we in the meanwhile make little effort to get through to it. The 'through' refers to the great body of extinct knowledge that has been acquired. The extinct knowledge is what we have compiled outside and from outside ourselves. But of course there is also the knowledge, the so-called knowledge, from inside ourselves, to which we might refer as inhuman knowledge, the source of man's inhumanity to man and to his environment. Knowledge from outside is unhuman just as knowledge from inside is inhuman.

Good spirit, by comparison, operates outwardly and inwardly, so that outside and inside ourselves is not open to it. Even more relevant is the fact that both outside and inside knowledge are what we have come up with in the first place in defence against and in opposition to good spirit. While our self-confidence and reliance on self is strong and great we wrongly suppose ourselves to be making great progress, and similarly while we are ignorant of how much of our energy originates in fear of the truth and of good spirit, we suppose ourselves to be making great strides ahead while in fact we only protect ourselves 'against the benevolent sheep at the door' to coin a phrase.

All this is well enough known, or at least suspected, I suppose, but acting upon that knowledge is not so easy because we have no tradition at our disposal. All that we have is what we have learned inclusive of personal experience and due to love of the truth. Out of our individual familiarity with good spirit we derive the confidence for inspired action, not from impersonal habits, routines and customs.

However everything we say can be twisted this way and that and our works must be such that they do us good whether others accept them or not.

As far as our mind is concerned, our mental receptivity and capacity, we are certainly at liberty to decide whether our brain should play a role or not. As soon as we decide that it should, a definite pressure is taken off us, as though we had found the lever that allows the dammed up water to propel the turbine rather than threatening to break the dam or to overflow. however we must understand that spirit in itself is unpredictable like the wind, while good spirit can be counted on to do us good even though we cannot predict the how, the where and the when of it.

The true progress is therefore from mere spirit to good spirit. The wilful harnessing of mere spirit is pointless and mostly disastrous. However once we have a mind, which is to say once we are able to think, to submit to 'thought-spirit', for the lack of a better word, we are well on our way to recognition or acknowledgment of good spirit. When we think, submitting to thought, we no longer insist on self-confidence because we learn to trust in that which is truly greater than our self. What we still need is to trust in that which is truly better than our self, inasmuch as it is good. Then we can give up so-called thought-systems and belief-systems, because we realize we are well cared for and taken care of.

*

What we need is a better definition and description of cerebration in comparison to thinking. When we think we give ourselves over to the spirit that is thought and in that spirit then we can thoughtfully express our relation to the world. Thinking is all to do with this relation to the world in which we stand. But we do not find ourselves in that relation. It does not simply occur to us. We have to think, so that we even recognize it and then perhaps draw assurance from it or even more important, delight and pleasure. True delight and real pleasure are gained thoughtfully, as we verify and realize our relation to the world. While we are ignorant of our relation to the world we are like orphans, feeling deprived of our natural heritage. We are puzzled then and ask: Why was I born into this world if in the last count it means nothing to me? I am forever struggling to find meaning for my existence but I find that what I touch turns to dust and what I do is never fruitful.

This is how we are, like lost souls who have to be forever busy so as not to feel condemned to a consciousness of insignificance. What our business gains us is a mock-world, a pretend-world, which actually has nothing to do with the real world except it stands between us and it.

The spirit which is thought is like a light that comes on in which we can appreciate the real world in which we are at home. When we think, we assent to this light, and the work we do in it, the thoughtful work, makes that light shine brightly also for others, so that those who are homeless might learn how to return to their home and to the world into which they were born.

So much for thinking. The organ of thought is the head. When we think we use our head as we tap into the spirit that is thought. Your head is naturally suited to cooperation with the spirit that is thought and to that peculiar activity which reveals to us how the world we actually live in cannot help but make meaningful sense to us and how the world that needs to be changed is a thing we have thoughtlessly allowed to crop up between ourselves and the real world. The real world obviously is not something that needs to be changed, just as our real life is not something that can be changed. The orphan who is forever wanting to change the world or to have his life changed remains in the orphanage.

While the head is the organ of thought, the brain is the organ of cerebration. When our brain suddenly makes its presence felt we may well experience a moment of panic. Certainly thought has to come to many but cerebration, which does not 'come' to anyone, like thought, is achieved by a few. They respond in a disciplined fashion to that characteristic initial panic by allowing themselves to be filled with good spirit which pours itself into them as soon as the preparation is complete. The emphasis here is not on relation to the real world but on personal wholeness.

*

Much has been written about this filling and fulfilling by spirit. What is not always clear is which spirit is meant. The 'holy spirit' presumably is the one that heals us and makes us whole. We have need of it at all times if we work and do not just sit on our hands. Our imagination is clarified and distinguished by holy spirit so that the world we imagine is no longer the one we have fabricated ourselves out of fear of the real world. At the same time this holy spirit cleanses our senses, so that the moods and emotions, the desires and passions welling up in us can be quickly identified and transformed, moods into mood, desires into desire and so on. It would not do to pretend that this teaching is for all. Those who are so to speak predestined human-naturally to teach and guide others, do themselves have this holy spirit as teacher and guide. They depend on him always and again to bring them back to the source of power and the origin of strength.

There is ample reason for referring to this healing spirit as a person. There is great temptation, especially during a materialistic age, to manipulate and control things, indeed to approach the world itself as a thing and as a collection of things. But things are immaterial and insignificant, which is why the materialist in us yearns for them. In truth things 'are not'. We cling to them as if they were beings, but beings cannot be manipulated and controlled. They are personal. Put it this way: things are the closest we can come to beings while indulging our materialistic habits of manipulation and control. In order to appreciate beings we must learn personal communication, which implies respect for the liberty and freedom of beings. As soon as we treat a being disrespectfully as a thing, we can no longer benefit from the healing strength and empowerment of the one we call the holy spirit.

So we must see to our own business and respectfully allow the holy spirit to see to 'his'. The distinction between personality and gender is difficult to make for some. It may help if we try to think of a person as a being that/who has entered into, or become involved in, communication, as in an exchange of live substance. However that's not quite right, is it. We have to distinguish between human beings and other beings. Human beings are capable of personality. We are able to respect and honour the liberty and freedom of all beings. Our reason for dong so is that we may know and understand beings in themselves. Love, for example, cannot be other than personal. As soon as we control and manipulate a being as if it were a thing, love has been displaced by fear. Love is honourable and respectful, that is all that that means.

Beings other than human beings cannot enter into communication of their own free will. It would not make sense to say that they can. What, are we to say then that the holy spirit we have referred to above is not personal?

In the past we have always managed to escape from this predicament by acknowledging that beings are created, while human beings are also created but essentially spiritual. Our minds, like our hearts, must in a sense be broken in order to make room for this, otherwise reason becomes monstrous and a tyrant. Just as the broken heart learns to know and to love, so the broken mind learns to believe and to behold. "Behold, I bring glad tidings," says the spirit, and "Believe in god. Believe also in me," says the spiritual human being. That which must remain mysterious to reason, is clearly revealed to faith. Insist on reason at the expense of faith and remain mystified. Insist on faith to the exclusion of reason and become fundamentalist or fanatical.

While people are popular creations, human beings are spiritual creations and open to personal communication with spirits. As people we are limited to communication with other people and inaccessible to good spirit but as human beings, by definition now, our personality involves us with personal spirits, from which we draw and receive all that is food, true, beautiful and strong.

*

I have demonstrated how reason alone cannot fully satisfy our human needs and desires. Neither of course can the answers of faith satisfy reason, but they can satisfy us. Once we have begun to live, in reality, we no longer find faith and reason as contradictory but we gladly benefit from both. We are not divided in ourself because we have a left hand and a right hand.

Reason alone is just as popular as faith alone, as we are discovering again in our own day. Mystification and zealotry are the two sides of the same false coin and we cannot rectify either one except by exemplifying the truth. If, in our misguided yearning for popularity, we are presented with mysteries, this seems to quieten and silence us for a while but then the worm of unhappiness stirs again, demanding clarity. If, on the other hand, we are presented with fanaticism, this seems to give us a sense of purpose for a while but then nihilism overshadows us again. The thirst for popularity can never be stilled. People will never be happy. As people we are misguided and mischievous. Therefore the search for the humanity in ourselves is well worth the effort.

*

Let's see what happens if we equate humanity, which is the essence of being, with this healing and whole-making spirit. Clearly we do not mean popular humanity, or, more simply, popularity. We mean the humanity we are born with. We stray from it or are misguided away from it, however we may return

38

to it. In that sense this spirit restores us to a previous wholeness. For example we search and strive for the wisdom that is not the wisdom of the expert specialist but that of children, especially little children.

Should we say, in that case, that in this healing spirit the humanity we have neglected and contradicted has come back to haunt us? Are little children in the possession of the whole-making spirit? Might that be why we, as comparatively ill adults, find them so affectionately attractive? Are we reminded of what we have forfeited and lost? Are we at times not angered and outraged by children because their much more complete humanity casts ours in the shade? Their reasons for saying what they say and for behaving as they do are not necessarily ours and the difference may be one of proximity to this healing spirit, the object of so much dispute and the subject of so much discussion but the fuel for not so much action.

Wisdom probably applies to nothing so much as to a human being's path from birth to maturity. Once we are ready to define properly, or to redefine, the term humanity as the essence of being and to admit the crucial difference between human beings and all other beings, we should have less trouble allowing for the spiritual dimension of all that truly is and has being. We should feel quite relaxed in our minds about saying that things are not, and that myths are not. When I honestly say that I am, I mean something specific, although this does not exclude me from the world of convention, which I may enter and leave again. As long as I keep in mind that the world of convention is not the real one. I may enter it to deliver messages, to set examples and to return again to the real world, frequently the worse for wear and therefore in need of healing.

If the spirit of healing and wholeness is not the one for me but instead the spirit of partiality and egotistic insistence on self-righteousness, I cannot enter the conventional world for the simple reason that I am not aware of it, as such or in comparison to a real world. Thankfully what happens most frequently, one hopes and assumes, is that the conventional world is chosen over the real one out of ignorance and not on account of rejection of the healing spirit.

With our mind alone we cannot grasp this notion of humanity as the essence of being and that whatever is, is human. Cerebration is required in addition to thought. It is by way of our brain, as the vital organ of cerebration, that healing spirit enters upon our constitution and into or field of vision. We cannot make it enter or tempt it to enter. What we can do is employ our brain organically and trust that this spirit cannot do other then be effective, on our behalf and on behalf of those we actively love, as soon as it physically can. When that will be and how soon, or how much, or when again, or in what manner if in some particular manner, is not possible for us to say, because just as all real beings are at liberty, so are all human beings free, precisely on account of the freedom originally exercised by this whole-making spirit.

Liberty could therefore be called the mode of freedom which beings other than human beings enjoy on account of their being essentially human. Human beings may enjoy freedom as such, which devolves upon us due to our exercise of personality and our practice of communality. In our popular pursuits we forfeit freedom and insist on liberty as such. In the possession of liberty we can do as we like but are limited in what we like. As human beings in possession of our freedom we can be as we wish and are limited in that we can only wish what is good for us.

*

At this stage it may seem as if we might achieve different results depending on whether we approach a subject mentally or by way of cerebration. If indeed this were the case we would have to take care to label what we come up with. Presumably the results of mental application must again be mentally perceived, while brain activity would be exclusively accessible to cerebration. However, while it is true that every new organ, new to ourselves, that is, has to be organized, which is to say organically perfected to a certain degree, in itself, its final perfection is not available until that organ is taken up into the sum total of our organic being. Thereafter that organ can still gain in unlimited diversity but its identity as that organ, available to us as such in unison with all our other organs, is complete.

We can, then, identify mental activity, essentially, and also brain activity, as such, and we know that long years of practice and application and performance are required not only before we can play a musical instrument as though it were an extension of or own flesh but also before we can properly think or use our brain. Just as bodily and mental activity need to be brought separately to a distinct pitch, so do mind and brain activity each have to be distinctly worked out, so that in a pinch we can say: Now I need to think a bit more, or: Now my brain activity has fallen behind. Compare it to a team of four, and you, the coachman, or the charioteer (in youth), have all your horses pulling in the same direction but now and again one of them overdoes it a bit or lags behind and then you apply the reign or the whip.

Traditionally intelligence and intellect pertain, respectively, to the mind and the brain, while instinct and intuition pertain to flesh and body. The match, however, is not just, if we look for it in terms of modern terminology, which at times seems to reveal that the language is more real than the speaker.

*

What we finally have to look at now is a peculiar teaching which links mind with flesh and brain with body.

Mentality is always acted out, we discussed that earlier. You recall how we said that mental activity is always visible. This is exemplified by the head being the visible organ of thinking. "He is using his head," we say, when we see someone ordering his affairs. We can tell how he goes about it. He places first things first and does not confuse bottom with top. The thinking he does is automatically illustrated. When we observe those who are especially gifted in their mind, we see them move and behave with the apparent confidence of a sleepwalker. Gifted sportsmen and sportswomen point to this link-up between mind and flesh, between mentality and carnality. The tennis player's thinking is quick and agile. The chess player thinks slowly and repetitiously. Sportsmen who perform their sport say to us: You can tell from my example how the human mind operates. I have a brain too, of course, but for the sake of demonstrating mental activity as such I keep my brain in abeyance. I am a mind and flesh specialist. I bring my gift to the altar, as the ancients used to say.

Activity due to the link-up of brain and body is not visible but invisible. Prayer, for example. No one can tell that you pray. You can do it anywhere, even in a church building. In fact there is no reason to cease from prayer. Your brain makes available the spiritual substance which your body requires in order to thrive in life. Compassionate cerebration – cerebral compassion: practice and exercise of the link-up between brain and body. The crisis is averted due to the link-up. What crisis? The possibility of 'brain-death', i.e. of classic stupidity on one hand, or of 'body death' on the other, such as classic aphasia. Any kind of critique (not criticism) is relevant up to the point of this link-up because both body and brain must be distinctly kept to the mark prior to it. Thereafter, with maturity, to use another word which signifies this coming together and joining up of disparate faculties and parts, reality is established.

We know that maturity can be approached from the stage of youth, naturally, or artificially from the state of immaturity. An immature adult may leave his state of immaturity by way of what we have elsewhere discussed as adult education. The youthful state, by comparison, would naturally culminate in mature adulthood, but under parental auspices. The immature adult must take himself in hand, while the child and the young man or woman require guidance.

It will become more apparent shortly how this theme is relevant here. Our main interest resides in this characteristic juncture of brain and body, of mind and flesh. We want to know what goes on on the other side, beyond the crisis. However we would never wish to close the door to true reality and we must not even talk as if that door could be closed, otherwise we become guilty of the worst hypocrisy. Consequently we have to describe, on one hand, the human-natural progression, in reality, from birth to mature adulthood, while on the other hand we realize how important it is to have practical means on hand for restoring our capacity for faithful loving and for extricating ourselves from mortal malpractices and the snares of selfishness.

So let us familiarize ourselves with both the natural crisis of youth on the final, critical stage prior to mature adulthood and the artificial crisis for which we ourselves can assume the responsibility because we have strayed into an immature state. I am suggesting that we remain aware of both these 'paths', as it were, so that our discussion of juncture, at the crossroads, so to speak, where our separately trained and educated faculties become mutually articulate, can remain close to practical experience and down-to-earth practice in the light of day. What we take in hand and undergo both reflects and advances our joyful living.

*

The natural path from youth to maturity and the artificial path from immaturity to maturity, these two shall occupy our attention now. We regard them from the point of view of adulthood. This means we are bound to view youth parentally and immaturity creatively.

On the surface these look like quite distinct operations. The parental adult is mature because he confesses his responsibility for those who are still young; in other words for children and youths.

Keep in mind that maturity must be maintained and sustained. As soon as we decide that the young are not our business we become immature in the sense that the parental component of the mature adult is ignored and lost by us.

Mature adults, we have said, are both parental and creative. When we stop being parental we become just as immature as when we stop being creative. The creativity that is required of us if we are to sustain our maturity is of course directed towards those who are no longer children or youths but adults and they are not yet or no longer mature. They have not sustained their maturity or they have not attained to it yet, in spite of the onset of adulthood.

I know that conventionally we equate adulthood with maturity. We might tell someone who acts the fool to behave like an adult. Thereby we imply that children are foolish and such a slur commonly suits the adult who wishes to wash his hands of his responsibility for children.

Similarly we equate immaturity with childishness and youthfulness, but this too is merely a conventional bias and we entertain it, I dare say, because we cannot be bothered to be creative towards the immature, thereby becoming as immature as the adult who will not engage parentally with children and youths.

Immaturity, therefore, is our lot, whether we give up our parental role or jettison our creative capacity. But immaturity is to be avoided at all costs. It involves guilt, regret, arrogance, presumptuousness and the like. All of these are life-negating. Negating these in turn, through repression or by way of self-justification, only makes matters worse. Life recedes from us and we wonder why.

*

Keeping in mind this difference between ourselves as immature adults and ourselves as parental and creative adults we should be able to make out what it is that allows us to call ourselves, or others, adults in the first place – but with reference to spirit and mind.

What we usually expect of adults is that they 'know their own mind'. They are aware of what they think; they are not swept away by a stream of thought but they remain aware. Adulthood implies self-consciousness within the context of our own being, so that we can allow others in our presence to think without half-consciously disputing their right to do so. What is remarkable at first when we use our heads is a degree of new freedom, of which we can be quite jealous. Anyone else who thinks – rather than merely falling in with our creativity – is liable to curtail our freedom, we feel. Such egotism of thought merely needs to be noticed, whereupon we become respectful again, as we learn that our thought-freedom must be passed on or shared rather than protected if we are to continue to enjoy the benefit of it.

The first thing the freely thinking adult has to learn, therefore, is to create bounds for his thinking and at the same time, by the same token, to respect the bounds of someone else's thinking.

In our youth we still depend on bounds set for our thinking by others, by so-called 'Society', or more legitimately by parental adults in whose care and under whose guidance we hopefully find ourselves. As an adult, by comparison, I ask myself such questions as: Why am I just thinking what I am thinking and do I wish to continue? If our thought is driven along a particular path we notice this and experience it as an infringement of our freedom. Spontaneous, not driven thought suits an adult. He frequently and repeatedly makes discoveries by way of thought because he insists on remaining within his chosen realm of mental activity.

I think as I choose to think, therefore I am an adult. Or, I am guided by the thought of others, as I choose to be guided, therefore I am young and youthful. For the adult it's as if a new light were being turned on when suddenly he realizes he can think or not think, as he sees fit.

The immature adult notices that he can no longer think as he would like to think. What he calls his passions, his emotions,

45

his moods and tempers, interferes with and cuts across his intentional thought paths. Nor can he allow himself to be guided by parental adults, as he did when he was young, because his ego will not allow this. Being immature, he 'has his pride'. Actually there is no way out for him by way of thought alone. This is because thought is initially a natural impulse, perhaps the most rigorously and purely natural impulse of all. Once our nature has been falsified, therefore, this impulse can no longer operate in freedom. We, in our turn, do well at this juncture to rely on artifice, or, as it is conventionally called, art.

Art is not natural but spiritual. We can imagine, consequently, how important a familiarity with spiritual values is when we have once again slipped into immaturity. But spiritual goods and values, as we know well enough by now, have to be learned. We have either been brought up to them or acquired them due to our own initiative.

It is when we set out, as immature adults, to avail ourselves of spiritual goods and values, to acquaint ourselves with them more nearly and to learn about them, that we can be helped by the mature adults in our vicinity. While we remain self-satisfied in our immaturity we cannot be helped.

The spirit of humility is good and valuable. As soon as we place ourselves within the confines of that spirit we signal to others that we are willing to be educated. This voluntary placing of ourselves within the confines of a good and valuable spirit can be seen as a kind of practice ground for when we will once again be able to think within responsible and disciplined bounds of our choice.

*

Modern man is not in the habit of distinguishing profitably between mind and spirit, between thinking and cerebrating, between head and brain. We do make distinctions, but usually in the service of some third category, so that the real marriage of mind and brain cannot come about. Not until we understand each on its own ground can we bring them together in unison.

Our way out of immaturity, in terms of educating and enlightenment, depends on our knowing the difference between natural being and learning. The fact that natural man, as we imagine him, has always reached for art and availed himself of devices in order to manage and cope should only encourage us in our assumption that something crucial is at stake here. Certainly immaturity can usefully be seen as a disjuncture of nature and art. When we insist on one at the expense of the other our immaturity becomes methodical and ingrained. If we sacrifice one to the other we mistake our immaturity for a higher, perhaps a sanctified or superlative maturity. In either case life becomes less and less available to us and our approach to the world and to our fellow man is unfortunate to say the least.

The ability to reach for a device when our natural faculties seem depleted depends to an extent on what we have learned up to that point in time. The corrective of education, specifically adult education, can therefore be seen as a healing of our natural being, just as art in general may be understood as the completion or perfection of our nature. All artificial devices, from the 'lowest' fetishist superstition to the 'highest' indwelling of and in merciful good spirit, if dispassionately – or perhaps we should say generously – viewed are, after all else is said and done, more or less successful ways of reaching out for more life and for a greater and more powerful quality of life.

*

Humility as a spirit – the spirit of humility : humility is not something we have to come up with in our natural self. We cannot come up with it there, only with substitutes or imitations. We pretend to be humble and wrongly call that humility. We imitate someone who is said to be humble. We are slavish, modest, timid and call that humility. It's modern fare and modern man gets far with his natural imitations. The point is that, far or

47

near, it does not get him where he wants to go. Spirits as such elude him. When he does look for them he insists they should wear fashionable garb. But let's not pick a quarrel with modern man. It would be too much like picking a quarrel with ourselves.

The spirit of light, of wakefulness and attentiveness, is another good and valuable spirit. How is it good? Inasmuch as it furthers life. How is it valuable? In that it sustains and begets strength.

So we have acquainted ourselves with two good and valuable spirits now, humility and clarity. Both are life-furthering. Both sustain and beget strength. That's a lot to be getting on with. We may ask ourselves: What does it practically mean to us that those spirits are available? Not much use to us if we merely know about them and do not give ourselves over to them or enlist them in our service. Actually we may do both of these at once – while we know what it is we do and why we do it.

*

You might say that we place ourselves within the sphere of influence of a spirit. We will then be motivated in accordance with that spirit. We will be influenced to be and do in a certain way.

Let's not pretend that this is something utterly foreign to our nature. The spirit of greed has often enough pulled our strings. We were greedy because it was a pleasure to be greedy. We were vengeful because it was a pleasure to be vengeful, a pleasure to be false, to be bad. Then we did things of which we were not particularly proud afterwards. We followed the spirit of deception, the spirit of hypocrisy, of arrogance. We followed these spirits because it made us feel more energetic, more in control. None of these spirits are good. None are valuable. Far from strengthening us, they undermine our humanity and waste our natural strength.

What is perhaps foreign to our nature is to persist in and abide by a spirit even though there is no immediate reward. As soon as we are forced to admit, by circumstances, that nothing appears to be different or to have changed due to our spiritual work, we leave off. This is of course a mistake. It takes practice to do the right thing and even more to do the good deed without having even one eye on the proceeds and the reward.

*

What difference could it possibly make that we speak of it as abiding in the confines of the spirit of greed, the spirit of humility, etc. rather than just plain saying we are humble or greedy? Is it not merely another way of looking at the same thing? Couldn't we just as readily describe it as a attitude of greed or humility, or as greedy or humble behaviour?

Quite correct, if what we have in mind is description and nothing more. In that case bad spirits may well have their way with us and we neither recognize them nor do we realize that suddenly we turn into a different being for a time. Only those around us are, often painfully, aware of it. And bad spirits do tend to occupy any space and time we leave for them. The parts of our body not occupied by good spirits will sooner or later be invaded and possessed by bad spirits. Sub specie aeternitatis this makes sense because it draws our attention, or at least it should if we have an ethical string to our bow, to those very 'spaces' which might give berth to good spirits. Then should begin the task of ejecting the bad while making room for the good.

When we say we abide within the confines of a spirit, this first of all emphasizes our activity, our being and doing. It's not just happening to us. "Oh dear, look at me, I'm greedy!" or "Look, I was quite humble there. How interesting!" – as a man without a soul would say, or a machine rather than a man. No, to abide implies a bit of intention, of effort. We have to be doing it and getting on with it. And we have to know what we are doing rather than blindly rattling ahead with some routine.

Then we abide 'within'. That is important, and telling. Ghosts may be hanging over us with their gray, killing seeming-presence but we abide, because we have good reason to do so, and we do so 'within', which implies that curious comfort imparted by good spirit when we cooperate with the presence of it.

There it is, all in one then: the abiding, the doing, the knowledge and comfort. Only question is: Are we doing it for the comfort? Are we abiding within whatever good spirit for the coincidental comfort we get from it?

If we did, the comfort would not last one minute. Try it and see. Rely on that coincidental comfort and see what happens. It disappears, of course. It's to help us on the way, not to draw us down by the side of it.

That Comforter has been talked about theologically at length. How nice, to be comforted while we go about the business of competitive survival, the routine and ambitious business of doing business, of making money, of keeping up with the Joneses! There, at least, we understand it as the accompanying comfort and not the narcissistic, self-centred comfort. That is something at least.

Now this is a very interesting question, for me at least, because I 'tend to overdo it'. I get overeager, when I'm on the scent of some spiritual success. But the immediate reward of hectic progress is not comfort but a lusty pleasure again. Before long I am working for that reward, of 'heightened existence'. Whereas the eternal accompanying comfort is, of course, not a reward at all but a help along the way and without that help I am bound to make hasty decisions and wrong moves. The accompanying comfort turns into a lusty reward. Too bad.

So: Yes, says the comforter, I shall stay with you while you head in the right direction but I cannot direct you. Of course you may take it as a hint, as a sign, if you no longer see me, or see me so clearly, but the change in tack, in speed, in purpose or whatever, is entirely up to you. This path we are taking is the path of utter freedom, of your freedom. How would you react if I curbed your liberty: you would insist on and persist in your error. Your historic tradition is a lengthy catalogue of freedom forfeited on account of liberty insisted upon or forcibly curbed. That's no way to get on.

*

So can I at least be sure that when I'm on the right track I have this comfort and when I'm on the wrong track I don't? And when I settle into that comfort as though it had been my aim or were my reward, I am as much on the wrong track as when I get addicted to motion and movement for its own sake because of the lusty pleasure it stands for?

I think so. Let's concentrate on working comfortably. I mean the eternal comfort, not soft cushions and plenty of diversion. Let's concentrate on abiding within good spirit and within good spirits. Spirit motivates and is motivation. The spirit I abide within (guaranteed a good spirit because it's impossible to abide within a bad spirit) motivates me, no doubt about that, whether I am aware of that right away or not.

This spirit of truth, for example is a fine motivation. You may abide within that spirit, comfortably, for some time before outward evidence shows. It definitely will, one way or another, you can take that for granted. The spirit of truth is rather central to the issue of work.

Did you know that the spirit of truth is available? Not a lot of people know that. As soon as we choose to abide within that spirit, comfortably, we may have to wait a while. However it's a wait only insofar as we equate recognizable results with results. Never has sheer discipline been so crucial.

*

Our works are inspired. They are inspired by the spirit in which we abide at the time. Good works are inspired by good spirit, bad works by bad spirit. Can we choose the spirit in which we wish to abide?

What if we were to abide in the messianic spirit? Would that frighten us at first? Much depends on how our mind has been

51

trained, both by ourselves, in line with experience and due to habit, and also by the various cultural agencies around us and active at our time of life.

It takes a certain kind of mind to perceive the messianic spirit, mainly because this spirit is all-embracing. The very mind which perceives it is altered by it, which is of course why most minds reject it. Those who are capable of abiding in this spirit have neither need nor wish ever to abide in any other spirit. They abide in it eternally and forever. It is the spirit that consummates all human endeavour. It makes no sense to teach anything about this spirit except insofar as it teaches itself. What it does to our mind is raise it up to its standard. It dictates its own logic. The simple issues of our everyday life are not ignored by it. Any purpose we come up with is included within the scope of it.

Truly the human mind strives for subsummation within the messianic spirit. What is the messianic spirit? It is that spirit in which the human mind, your mind and my mind, desires to come to rest. Until it does, it searches this way and that, it attempts and experiments, it builds and tears down.

Then our thinking is thrown back upon itself as illusory and we are forced to distance ourselves from our mental processes. We are forced to confess that only what we can think within the messianic spirit is really worth thinking. The real favour we can now do ourselves is to accept this scenario with good grace. While we fight force with force we, as it were, only anger the elements.

After a time the messianic limitation reveals itself as necessary for perfection. When we think now we no longer organize what we are going to think ahead of time but we think spontaneously. Such thought automatically abides within the confines of the messianic spirit. While we know this we cannot go wrong.

* * * * *   (9,09,2005)

www.ingramcontent.com/pod-product-compliance
Lightning Source LLC
Chambersburg PA
CBHW070332290526
45791CB00003B/1306